Quick & Easy Indian Cooking

Quick & Easy Indian Cooking

LOUISE STEELE

SHOOTING STAR PRESS

This edition printed in 1995 for:
Shooting Star Press Inc
230 Fifth Avenue – Suite 1212
New York, NY 10001

Shooting Star Press books are available at special discounts for bulk purchases for sales promotions,
premiums, fund-raising, or educational use. Special edition or book excerpts can also be created to
specification. For details contact: Special Sales Director, Shooting Star Press Inc., 230 Fifth Avenue,
Suite 1212, New York, NY 10001

© Parragon Book Service Ltd 1994

ISBN 1 56924 190 2

Printed in Italy

Acknowledgements:

Design & DTP: Pedro & Frances Prá-Lopez / Kingfisher Design
Art Direction: Clive Hayball
Managing Editor: Alexa Stace
Special Photography: Amanda Hayward
Home Economist: Nicola Fowler
Stylist: Marion Price

Gas Hob supplied by New World Domestic Appliances Ltd
Photographs on pages 6, 18, 30, 52 & 64: By courtesy of ZEFA

Contents

CHAPTER ONE

Appetizers

Whether you are planning a full-scale dinner party, an informal buffet or a nourishing family meal, don't forget to include a few appetizers to tempt the tastebuds at the start of the meal. Appetizers or hors d'oeuvres are not generally served as such on the Indian menu, but dishes like chicken tikka, tiger prawns or spicy mini kebabs make for a typical beginning. Use hot spices cautiously in such palate-enticing dishes, and serve with a yogurt and cucumber cool dipping sauce.

Alternatively, do as the Indians do and serve a selection of snack foods like bhajis and pakoras before the main meal – they are perfect finger food to serve with drinks.

Rarely are soups served at an authentic meal – they are not considered to be traditional Indian cuisine: they are something the Indians have copied from the English since the days of the Raj.

Opposite: *A bustling scene at Crawford Market in Bombay.*

STEP 1

STEP 2

STEP 4

STEP 5

SHRIMP POORIS

Tiger prawns are especially good cooked this way, although the less expensive, smaller shelled jumbo shrimp may be used instead.

SERVES 6

POORIS:
½ cup whole-wheat flour
½ cup all-purpose flour
1 tbsp ghee or vegetable oil
2 good pinches of salt
5 tbsp hot water

TOPPING:
½ lb fresh spinach, washed and stems trimmed
4 tbsp ghee or vegetable oil, plus extra oil for shallow frying
1 onion, peeled and chopped
1 garlic clove, peeled and crushed
½-1 tsp minced chili (from a jar)
1-1½ tbsp medium curry paste, to taste
1 cup canned chopped tomatoes
⅔ cup coconut milk
½ lb shelled raw tiger prawns or jumbo shrimp

1 To make the pooris, put the flours in a bowl and make a well in the center. Add the ghee or oil, salt and hot water and mix to form a dough. Leave to stand for 1 hour.

2 Meanwhile, prepare the topping. Cut the spinach crosswise into wide strips – do this by making bundles of leaves and slicing with a sharp knife.

3 Heat the ghee or oil in a skillet, add the onion, garlic, chili and spinach and cook gently for 4 minutes, shaking the skillet and stirring frequently. Add the curry paste, tomatoes and coconut milk and simmer for 10 minutes, stirring occasionally. Remove from the heat, stir in the prawns or shrimp and season with salt to taste.

4 Knead the dough well on a floured surface, divide into 6 pieces and shape into 6 balls. Roll out each one into a 5 in circle. Heat about 1 in oil in a deep skillet until smoking hot. Take one poori at a time, lower it into the hot oil and cook for 10-15 seconds on each side until puffed up and golden. Remove the poori with a slotted spoon, drain on paper towels and keep warm while cooking the remainder in the same way.

5 Reheat the prawn or shrimp mixture, stirring until piping hot. Arrange a poori on each serving plate and spoon the prawn or shrimp and spinach mixture onto each one. Serve immediately.

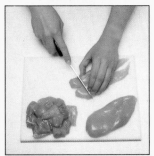

STEP 1

STEP 2

STEP 3

STEP 4

SPICY CHICKEN TIKKA

Serve these tasty kebabs on a bed of finely shredded crisp lettuce, slivered onion and grated eating apple drizzled with a little lemon or lime juice.

SERVES 6

1 lb boneless chicken breast halves, skinned
salt and freshly ground black pepper
1½ tbsp tikka curry paste (from a jar)
6 tbsp plain yogurt
1 tbsp lemon juice
½ onion, peeled and finely chopped
1½ tbsp chopped chives or scallion leaves
1½ tbsp finely chopped gingerroot
1-2 garlic cloves, peeled and crushed
1½ tbsp sesame seeds
2 tbsp vegetable oil
wedges of lemon or lime, to garnish

1 Cut the chicken into small bite-sized pieces, place in a shallow glass dish and season with salt and pepper to taste.

2 In a small bowl, mix together the remaining ingredients, except the sesame seeds and oil, and pour over the chicken. Mix well until all the chicken pieces are coated, then cover and refrigerate for at least 1 hour, or for longer if possible.

3 Thread the chicken pieces onto 6 bamboo or metal skewers and sprinkle with the sesame seeds.

4 Place on a rack in a broiler pan and drizzle with the oil. Cook under a hot broiler for about 15 minutes, or until cooked through and browned, turning frequently and brushing with more oil, if necessary. Serve hot, garnished with wedges of lemon or lime.

HELPFUL HINTS

To prevent bamboo skewers from charring during cooking, soak them in cold water for 30 minutes before threading with the chicken.

MINTED ONION BHAJIS

Gram flour (also known as besan flour) is used here to make the bhajis. It is a fine yellow flour made from ground chick-peas and is available from Asian grocery stores and some health-food stores.

STEP 1

MAKES 12

1 cup gram flour
¼ tsp cayenne pepper
¼-½ tsp ground cilantro
¼-½ tsp ground cumin
1 tbsp chopped fresh mint
salt and freshly ground black pepper
4 tbsp plain yogurt
¼ cup cold water
1 large onion, peeled, quartered and thinly sliced
vegetable oil, for frying
mint sprigs, to garnish

turning frequently. Drain on paper towels and keep warm while cooking the remainder in the same way. Serve hot or warm.

STEP 2

1 Put the gram flour into a bowl, add the cayenne pepper, cilantro, cumin and mint and season with salt and pepper to taste. Stir in the yogurt, water and sliced onion and mix well together.

2 One-third fill a large, deep skillet with oil and heat until hot. Drop heaped spoonfuls of the mixture, a few at a time, into the hot oil and use 2 forks to neaten the mixture into rough ball shapes.

3 Fry the bhajis until rich golden brown and cooked through,

STEP 3a

VARIATION

For a more fiery flavor, add 1 seeded and chopped fresh green chili (or 1 teaspoon ready prepared minced chili, from a jar) to the above ingredients and omit the cayenne pepper, if wished.

STEP 3b

STEP 1a

STEP 1b

STEP 2

STEP 3

LAMB & TOMATO KOFTAS

These little meatballs, served with a minty yogurt dressing, can be prepared well in advance, ready to cook when required.

SERVES 4

½ lb finely ground lean lamb
1½ onions, peeled
1-2 garlic cloves, peeled and crushed
1 dried red chili, finely chopped (optional)
2-3 tsp garam masala
2 tbsp chopped fresh mint
2 tsp lemon juice
salt
2 tbsp vegetable oil
4 small tomatoes, quartered
mint sprigs, to garnish

YOGURT DRESSING:
²⁄₃ cup plain yogurt
2 in piece cucumber, grated
2 tbsp chopped fresh mint
½ tsp toasted cumin seeds (optional)

1 Place the ground lamb in a bowl. Finely chop 1 onion and add to the bowl with the garlic and chili, if using. Stir in the garam masala, mint and lemon juice and season well with salt. Mix the ingredients together well. Divide the mixture in half, then divide each half into 10 equal portions and form each into a small ball. Roll balls in the oil to coat. Quarter the remaining onion half and separate into layers.

2 Thread 5 of the balls, 4 tomato quarters and some of the onion layers onto each of 4 bamboo or metal skewers. Brush the vegetables with the remaining oil and cook under a hot broiler for about 10 minutes, turning frequently until they are browned all over and cooked through.

3 Meanwhile, prepare the yogurt dressing. Mix the yogurt with the cucumber, mint and toasted cumin seeds, if using. Garnish the lamb koftas with mint sprigs and serve hot with the yogurt dressing.

SHAPING KOFTAS

It is important that the lamb is finely ground and the onion finely chopped or the mixture will not shape neatly and easily into balls. The mixture can be finely processed in a food processor, if wished.

STEP 1

STEP 3

STEP 4a

STEP 4b

PAKORAS

These vegetable fritters are simple to make and extremely good to eat.
They may be served as a first course or as an accompaniment
to a main course.

SERVES 4-6

4 oz broccoli
1 onion
2 potatoes
1¹/₂ cups gram flour
1 tsp garam masala
1¹/₂ tsp salt
¹/₂ tsp cayenne pepper
1 tsp cumin seeds
scant 1 cup water
vegetable oil, for deep frying
cilantro sprigs, to garnish

1 Cut the broccoli into small flowerets, discarding most of the stem, then cook in a saucepan of boiling, salted water for 4 minutes. Drain well, return to the pot and shake dry over a low heat for a few moments. Place the broccoli on paper towels to completely dry while preparing the other vegetables.

2 Peel and thinly slice the onion and separate into rings. Peel and thinly slice the potatoes and pat dry.

3 Place the gram flour in a bowl with the garam masala, salt, cayenne pepper and cumin seeds. Make a well in the center, add the water and mix to form a smooth batter.

4 One-third fill a deep-fat fryer or saucepan with oil and heat to 375°F, or until a cube of day-old bread browns in 30 seconds. Dip the vegetables into the batter to coat, then lower into the hot oil and fry, in batches, for 3-4 minutes, or until golden brown and crisp. Drain on paper towels and keep warm while cooking the remainder in the same way. Serve the pakoras hot, garnished with cilantro sprigs.

VARIATIONS

Small cauliflower flowerets, strips of red or green bell pepper and slices of zucchini are also very good cooked this way. The cauliflower should be parboiled in the same way as broccoli (see step 1) before dipping in the batter. Use up the leftover broccoli (or cauliflower) stems in a soup, rice or a main course dish.

CHAPTER TWO

Fish

At first glance India may not be considered to be a great fish-eating nation, but there are some parts of it, notably Bengal and around Karachi, where fish is very popular and consequently plays a very important part in the diet. Indeed India has a coastline stretching for over 2,500 miles and with internal waters can supply over 2,000 varieties of fish!

Many fish and shellfish are simply broiled, whole or on skewers, after sprinkling with a few spices and brushing with mustard oil; others are fried whole or as fish and vegetable fritters; some with a firm, meaty texture, like cod, are curried in aromatic sauces and frequently flavored with coconut. Countless others are baked, steamed, poached or roasted with that characteristic Indian flavor that is based on a marsala of spices that enhances, but does not overwhelm, the delicate flavor of the fish.

Opposite: *Pushkar Lake, Rajasthan. Both freshwater fish and seafood play a large part in the cooking styles of India.*

STEP 1a

STEP 1b

STEP 2

STEP 3

SHRIMP& CHILI SAUCE

Quick and easy to prepare and extremely good to eat. Use the large and succulent tiger prawns for special occasions, when the budget is not a consideration.

SERVES 4

4 tbsp ghee or vegetable oil
1 onion, peeled, quartered and sliced
1 bunch scallions, trimmed and sliced
1 garlic clove, peeled and crushed
1-2 fresh green chilies, seeded and finely
    chopped
1-in piece gingerroot, finely chopped
1 tsp ground turmeric
1 tsp ground cumin
1 tsp ground cilantro
1½ tsp curry powder or paste
1 x 14-oz can chopped tomatoes
⅔ cup water
⅔ cup heavy cream
1 lb shelled shrimp
1-2 tbsp chopped fresh cilantro
salt
cilantro sprigs, to garnish

1 Heat the ghee or vegetable oil in a saucepan and fry the onion and scallions, garlic and chili over gentle heat for 3 minutes. Stir in the ginger, spices and curry powder or paste and cook very gently for a further 1 minute, stirring all the time.

2 Stir in the tomatoes and water and bring to a boil, stirring. Reduce the heat and simmer for 10 minutes, stirring occasionally.

3 Add the cream, mix well and simmer for 5 minutes, then add the shrimp and cilantro and season with salt to taste. Cook gently for 2-3 minutes. Taste and adjust the seasoning, if necessary. Serve garnished with cilantro sprigs.

PREPARING EARLY

This dish may be prepared in advance to the end of step 2. A few minutes before the dish is required for serving, reheat the mixture until simmering, then follow the instructions given in step 3.

INDIAN BROILED TROUT

Here is a deliciously simple way of preparing and cooking trout.
It is also good with nice fresh, plump mackerel.

STEP 1

SERVES 4

4 trout, each weighing about ¹/₂ lb, dressed
salt
6 tbsp ghee or melted butter
1-2 garlic cloves, peeled and crushed
1 fresh green chili, seeded and chopped, or
  use 1 tsp minced chili (from a jar)
1-in piece gingerroot, peeled and finely
  chopped
1¹/₂ tsp cumin seeds
1 tsp garam masala
1 tsp ground cumin
finely grated rind of 1 lemon
juice of 2 lemons
cilantro sprigs and lemon wedges, to garnish

3 Spoon half the mixture over the trout and cook under a moderately hot broiler for 5-8 minutes, or until cooked on one side. Turn the fish over and spoon the remaining mixture over the fish and broil for a further 5-8 minutes, basting with the juices in pan during cooking.

4 Arrange the trout on a hot serving plate, spoon the pan juices over the fish and garnish with cilantro sprigs and lemon wedges. Serve hot.

STEP 2a

STEP 2b

1 Using a sharp knife, carefully make 3 diagonal slashes (not too deep) on each side of the trout. Season the trout and place in a lightly greased broiler pan.

2 Melt the ghee or butter in a small saucepan over a low heat, add the crushed garlic, chili, chopped ginger and spices and cook very gently for 30 seconds, stirring. Remove the pan from the heat and stir the lemon rind and juice into the mixture.

SLASHING THE TROUT

Take care when making the diagonal slashes on each side of the trout not to cut too deeply or you will cut into the bones and spoil the finished result.

STEP 3

STEP 1

STEP 2

STEP 3

STEP 4

SPICY FISH & POTATO FRITTERS

You need floury-textured main crop potatoes for making these tasty fritters. Any white fish of your choice may be used.

SERVES 4

3 cups potatoes, peeled and cut into even-sized pieces
1 lb white fish fillets, such as cod or haddock, skinned and boned
6 scallions, sliced
1 fresh green chili, seeded
2 garlic cloves, peeled
1 tsp salt
1 tbsp medium or hot curry paste
2 eggs, beaten
2¹/₂ cups fresh white bread crumbs
vegetable oil, for shallow frying
lime wedges and cilantro sprigs, to garnish
mango chutney, to serve

1 Cook the potatoes in a saucepan of boiling, salted water until tender. Drain well, return the potatoes to the pot and place over a moderate heat for a few moments to dry off. Cool slightly, then place in a food processor with the fish, scallions, chili, garlic, salt and curry paste. Process until the ingredients are very finely chopped and blended.

2 Turn the potato mixture into a bowl and mix in 2 tablespoons of beaten egg and 1 cup of bread crumbs. Place the remaining beaten egg and bread crumbs in separate dishes.

3 Divide the fish mixture into 8 and, using a spoon to help you (the mixture is quite soft), dip first in the beaten egg and then coat in the bread crumbs, and carefully shape the mixture into ovals.

4 Heat enough oil in a large skillet for shallow frying and fry the fritters over medium heat for 3-4 minutes, turning frequently, until golden brown and cooked through. Drain on paper towels and garnish with lime wedges and cilantro sprigs. Serve hot, with mango chutney.

FRITTERS

Make these fish fritters more or less fiery by increasing or reducing the amount of chili, as wished. For really speedy fritters, simply drop spoonfuls of the egg and crumbed fish mixture into the hot fat and, using a metal spatula, pat into rough shapes during cooking.

SEAFOOD & AROMATIC RICE

One of those easy, delicious meals where the rice and fish are cooked together in one pan. The whole spices are not meant to be eaten: they flavor the dish during cooking and should be removed before serving.

STEP 1

SERVES 4

1¼ cups basmati rice
2 tbsp ghee or vegetable oil
1 onion, peeled and chopped
1 garlic clove, peeled and crushed
1 tsp cumin seeds
½-1 tsp chili powder
4 cloves
1 cinnamon stick or a piece of cassia bark
2 tsp curry paste
½ lb shelled shrimp
1 lb white fish fillets (such as monkfish, cod or haddock), skinned and boned and cut into bite-sized pieces
salt and freshly ground black pepper
2½ cups boiling water
⅓ cup frozen peas
⅓ cup frozen whole-kernel corn
1-2 tbsp lime juice
2 tbsp toasted shredded coconut
cilantro sprigs and lime slices, to garnish

1 Place the rice in a strainer and wash well under cold running water until the water runs clear, then drain well. Heat the ghee or oil in a saucepan, add the onion, garlic, spices and curry paste and fry very gently for 1 minute.

2 Stir in the rice and mix well until coated in the spiced oil. Add the shrimp and white fish and season well with salt and pepper. Stir lightly, then stir in the boiling water.

STEP 2

3 Cover and cook gently for 10 minutes, without uncovering the pot. Add the peas and corn, cover and continue cooking for a further 8 minutes. Remove from the heat and allow to stand for 10 minutes.

4 Uncover the pot, fluff up the rice with a fork and transfer to a warm serving platter. Sprinkle the dish with the lime juice and toasted coconut, and serve garnished with cilantro sprigs and lime slices.

STEP 3

VARIATION

For yellow rice, add ½ teaspoon ground turmeric to the pot together with the other spices at step 1. Alternatively, to add flavor as well as color to the dish, omit the turmeric and add 2 good pinches of toasted and crushed saffron strands instead.

STEP 4

STEP 1

STEP 2

STEP 3a

STEP 3b

INDIAN COD WITH TOMATOES

Quick and easy – cod steaks are cooked in a rich tomato and coconut sauce to produce tender, succulent results. You can, of course, use any firm white fish available instead of cod.

SERVES 4

3 tbsp vegetable oil
4 cod steaks, about 1 in thick
salt and freshly ground black pepper
1 onion, peeled and finely chopped
2 garlic cloves, peeled and crushed
1 red bell pepper, seeded and chopped
1 tsp ground cilantro
1 tsp ground cumin
1 tsp ground turmeric
$^1/_2$ tsp garam masala
1 x 14-oz can chopped tomatoes
$^2/_3$ cup coconut milk
1-2 tbsp chopped fresh cilantro or parsley

1 Heat the oil in a skillet, add the fish steaks, season with salt and pepper and fry until browned on both sides (but not cooked through). Remove from the skillet and reserve.

2 Add the onion, garlic, red bell pepper and spices and cook very gently for 2 minutes, stirring frequently. Add the tomatoes, bring to a boil and simmer for 5 minutes.

3 Return the fish steaks to the skillet and simmer gently for 8 minutes or until the fish is cooked through. Remove from the skillet and keep warm on a serving dish. Add the coconut milk and cilantro to the skillet and reheat gently. Spoon the sauce over the cod steaks and serve immediately.

VARIATIONS

The mixture may be flavored with a tablespoonful of curry powder or curry paste (mild, medium or hot, according to personal preference) instead of the mixture of spices at step 2, if wished.

CHAPTER THREE

Meat & Poultry

Curries are, of course, the most famous of the Indian meat dishes, but they are by no means the only dishes the Indian culinary repertoire has to offer! Consider stir-fries with a blend of Indian spices, skewered kebabs of meat and vegetables, vegetables stuffed with savory meat and rice or lentil mixtures, risotto-style combinations of meat with rice, or meat roasted tandoori-style.

Even then there are differences and variations which give a typical national dish a distinctive regional flavor all of its own. South Indian curries, for example, are fierce and fiery, while North Kashmiri and Punjab meat dishes are mild and strongly flavored with onion and garlic. Western or Goan dishes are slow-cooked, hot and thickened with coconut milk, whereas Eastern meat dishes rely upon spices like mustard, cumin and anise for their distinctive flavor and originality.

Opposite: Unloading supplies on the banks of the Ganges, in the holy city of Benares.

STEP 1a

STEP 1b

STEP 2a

STEP 2b

CHICKEN WITH SPICY CHICK-PEAS

This is a delicious combination of chick-peas and chicken flavored with fragrant spices. Using canned chick-peas (rather than the dried ones) speeds up the cooking time considerably.

SERVES 4

3 tbsp ghee or vegetable oil
8 small chicken portions, such as thighs or
  drumsticks
1 large onion, peeled and chopped
2 garlic cloves, peeled and crushed
1-2 fresh green chilies, seeded and chopped,
  or use 1-2 tsp minced chili (from a jar)
2 tsp ground cumin
2 tsp ground cilantro
1 tsp garam masala
1 tsp ground turmeric
1 x 14-oz can chopped tomatoes
²/₃ cup water
1 tbsp chopped fresh mint
1 x 15-oz can chick-peas, drained
salt
1 tbsp chopped fresh cilantro
plain yogurt, to serve (optional)

1 Heat the ghee or oil in a large saucepan and fry the chicken pieces all over until sealed and lightly golden. Remove from the pot. Add the onion, garlic, chili and spices and cook very gently for 2 minutes, stirring frequently.

2 Stir in the tomatoes, water, mint and chick-peas. Mix well, return the chicken portions to the pot, season with salt to taste, then cover and simmer gently for about 20 minutes or until the chicken is tender and cooked through.

3 Taste and adjust the seasoning if necessary, then sprinkle with the chopped cilantro and serve hot, drizzled with yogurt, if using.

VARIATIONS

Canned black-eyed peas and red kidney beans also make delicious additions to this spicy chicken dish. Be sure to drain the canned beans and to rinse them, if necessary, before adding to the pan.

STEP 1

STEP 2a

STEP 2b

STEP 3

CHICKEN IN SPICED COCONUT

This delicious combination makes a perfect dinner-party course – and what's more it is quick and simple to prepare.

SERVES 4

4 boneless chicken breast halves, skinned
6 tbsp vegetable oil
2 onions, peeled, quartered and thinly sliced
1 garlic clove, peeled and crushed
1 in piece fresh gingerroot, peeled and finely
    chopped
1-2 fresh green chilies, seeded and finely
    chopped, or use 1-2 tsp minced chili (in a
    jar)
2 1/2 cups mushrooms, wiped and sliced
2 tsp medium curry powder
2 tsp ground cilantro
1/2 tsp ground cinnamon
1 tbsp sesame seeds
2/3 cup chicken stock or water
1 cup canned chopped tomatoes
1 1/4 cups coconut milk
salt
cilantro sprigs, to garnish

1 Cut each chicken breast half into 3 diagonal pieces. Heat 4 tablespoons of oil in a saucepan and fry the chicken pieces until lightly sealed all over. Remove from the pot and reserve.

2 Add the remaining oil to the pot and gently fry the onions, garlic, ginger, chilies, mushrooms, curry powders, spices and sesame seeds for 3 minutes, stirring frequently. Stir in the chicken stock, tomatoes and coconut milk. Season with salt to taste and bring to a boil.

3 Reduce the heat, return the chicken pieces to the pan and simmer gently, uncovered, for about 12 minutes, or until the chicken is tender and cooked through and the sauce has thickened, stirring occasionally. Garnish with cilantro sprigs.

S P I C E S

Increase the pungency of the mixture by adding more curry powder or chili, to taste. You can also leave the dish to stand overnight to allow the flavors to develop and reheat it gently when required.

CHICKEN & AROMATIC ALMONDS

Rich and delicious – enjoy the succulence of chicken cooked with yogurt, cream and ground almonds flavored with aromatic garam masala.

SERVES 4

²/₃ cup plain yogurt
¹/₂ tsp cornstarch
4 tbsp ghee or vegetable oil
4 boneless chicken breast halves
2 onions, peeled and sliced
1 garlic clove, peeled and crushed
1 in piece fresh gingerroot, peeled and
    chopped
1¹/₂ tbsp garam masala
¹/₂ tsp chili powder
2 tsp medium curry paste
1¹/₄ cups chicken stock
salt and freshly ground black pepper
²/₃ cup heavy cream
¹/₂ cup blanched almonds, finely ground
1 cup thin green beans, topped, tailed and
    halved
juice of ¹/₂ lemon
toasted slivered almonds, to garnish
boiled rice, to serve

1 Smoothly blend the yogurt in a
small bowl with the cornstarch.
Heat the ghee or oil in a large flameproof
casserole, add the chicken breast halves
and fry until golden all over. Remove the
chicken from the casserole and reserve.

2 Add the onions, garlic and ginger
to the casserole and fry gently for 3

minutes, then add the garam masala,
chili powder and curry paste and fry
gently for 1 minute. Stir in the stock,
yogurt and salt and pepper to taste and
bring to a boil, stirring all the time.

3 Return the chicken pieces to the
casserole, then cover and simmer
gently for 25 minutes. Remove the
chicken to a dish and keep warm.

4 Blend the cream with the ground
almonds and add to the sauce, then
stir in the green beans and lemon juice
and boil vigorously for 1 minute, stirring
all the time.

5 Return the chicken to the
casserole, cover and cook gently for
a further 10 minutes. Serve with rice and
garnish with toasted slivered almonds.

ALTERNATIVE

Chicken portions may be used instead of
breasts, if preferred, and should be cooked
for 10 minutes longer at step 3.

STEP 1

STEP 2

STEP 3

STEP 4

STIR-FRY CHICKEN CURRY

A tasty mix of chicken, peppers and cashew nuts is stir-fried with spices to give a delicious dish in minutes.

SERVES 4

4 boneless chicken breast halves, skinned
6 tbsp plain yogurt
juice of 1 lime
2 garlic cloves, peeled and crushed
2 in piece gingerroot, peeled and chopped
2 tbsp medium or hot curry paste, to taste
1 tbsp paprika
salt
5 tbsp ghee or vegetable oil
1 onion, peeled, quartered and separated into layers
1 red bell pepper, seeded and cut into ½-in pieces
1 green bell pepper, seeded and cut into ½-in pieces
½ cup unsalted cashews
4 tbsp water
snipped chives or scallion leaves, to garnish

1 Cut the chicken breast halves into ½-in wide strips and place in a bowl. Add the yogurt, lime juice, garlic, ginger, curry paste and paprika. Season well and mix the ingredients together.

2 Heat the ghee or oil in a large skillet, add the onion, red and green bell peppers and the cashews and stir-fry over a moderate heat for 2

minutes. Remove from the skillet and reserve.

3 Stir the chicken mixture into the skillet and stir-fry for 4-5 minutes until well sealed and cooked though.

4 Add the water and mix well, then return the vegetables to the skillet, reduce the heat and cook gently for 2 minutes. Serve at once, sprinkled with chives or scallion leaves.

VARIATIONS

Thin strips of pork tenderloin or sirloin steak are also extremely good cooked this way. Add slices of zucchini or celery instead of one of the bell peppers, if wished, and substitute blanched almonds for the cashews.

CHICKEN & VEGETABLE RICE

Boneless chicken meat may be used here instead of the drumsticks, if preferred. In which case slash them diagonally through the skin and into the flesh to allow the flavors of the sauce to penetrate.

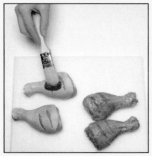

STEP 1

STEP 3a

STEP 3b

STEP 4

SERVES 4-6

4 chicken drumsticks
3 tbsp mango chutney
1½ tbsp lemon juice
6 tbsp vegetable oil
1½-2 tbsp medium or hot curry paste
1½ tsp paprika
1 large onion, peeled and chopped
1½ cups button mushrooms, wiped and left whole
2 carrots, peeled and thinly sliced
2 celery stalks, trimmed and thinly sliced
½ eggplant, quartered and sliced
2 garlic cloves, peeled and crushed
½ tsp ground cinnamon
1¼ cups long-grain rice
2½ cups chicken stock or water
½ cup frozen peas or sliced green beans
⅓ cup seedless raisins
salt and freshly ground black pepper
wedges of hard-boiled egg and lemon slices, to garnish (optional)

1 Slash the drumsticks twice on each side, cutting through the skin and deep into the flesh each time. Mix the chutney with the lemon juice, 1 tablespoon oil, curry paste and paprika. Brush over the drumsticks and reserve the remainder.

2 Heat 2 tablespoons of oil in the skillet and fry the drumsticks over a moderate heat for about 5 minutes until sealed and golden brown all over.

3 Meanwhile, heat the remaining oil in a saucepan, add the onion, mushrooms, carrots, celery, eggplant, garlic and cinnamon and fry lightly for 1 minute. Stir in the rice and cook gently for 1 minute, stirring until the rice is well coated with the oil. Add the stock and the remaining mango chutney mixture, peas, raisins and salt and pepper to taste. Mix well and bring to a boil.

4 Reduce the heat and add the drumsticks to the mixture, pushing them down into the liquid. Cover and cook gently for 25 minutes until the liquid has been absorbed, the drumsticks are tender and the rice is cooked.

5 Remove the drumsticks from the pan and keep warm. Fluff up the rice mixture and transfer to a warm serving plate. Arrange the rice into a nicely shaped mound and place the drumsticks around it. Garnish the dish with wedges of hard-boiled egg and lemon slices, if using.

BEEF & MUSHROOM CURRY

Vary the meat here according to personal taste, using lean lamb or pork (leg or shoulder cuts are ideal) instead of beef. Omit the finishing touches in step 4, if wished.

STEP 1

SERVES 4

1½ lb lean braising beef, trimmed
3 tbsp vegetable oil
2 onions, peeled, quartered and sliced
2 garlic cloves, peeled and crushed
1-in piece gingerroot, peeled and chopped
2 fresh green chilies, seeded and chopped, or
    use 1-2 tsp minced chili (from a jar)
1½ tbsp medium curry paste
1 tsp ground cilantro
2½-3½ cups mushrooms, thickly sliced
3½ cups stock or water
3 tomatoes, chopped
½-1 tsp salt
⅓ cup creamed coconut, chopped
2 tbsp blanched almonds, finely ground

TO FINISH:
2 tbsp vegetable oil
1 green or red bell pepper, seeded and cut
    into thin strips
6 scallions, trimmed and sliced
1 tsp cumin seeds

1 Cut the beef into small bite-sized cubes. Heat the oil in a saucepan, add the beef and fry until sealed, stirring frequently. Remove from the pot.

2 Add the onions, garlic, ginger, chilies, curry paste and cilantro to the pot and cook gently for 2 minutes. Stir in the mushrooms, stock and tomatoes and season with salt to taste. Return the beef to the pot, then cover and simmer very gently for 1¼-1½ hours or until beef is tender.

STEP 2

3 Stir the chopped creamed coconut and ground almonds into the curry, then cover the pan and cook gently for 3 minutes.

4 Meanwhile, heat the remaining oil in a skillet, add the bell pepper strips and scallion slices and fry gently until glistening and tender-crisp. Stir in the cumin seeds and fry gently for 30 seconds, then spoon the mixture over the curry and serve at once.

STEP 3

PREPARATION

You will find this dish is even tastier if made the day before because this allows time for the flavors to blend and develop. Make the curry to the end of step 3, cool and store in the refrigerator until required. Reheat it gently until piping hot before adding the finishing touches.

STEP 4

43

STEP 1

STEP 2

STEP 3

STEP 4

PORK CHOPS & SPICY RED BEANS

A substantial dish that is packed full of goodness. The spicy bean mixture, served on its own, also makes a good accompaniment to meat or chicken dishes.

SERVES 4

3 tbsp ghee or vegetable oil
4 pork chops, skin and fat removed
2 onions, peeled and thinly sliced
2 garlic cloves, peeled and crushed
2 fresh green chilies, seeded and chopped or
    use 1-2 tsp minced chili (from a jar)
1-in piece gingerroot, peeled and chopped
1$\frac{1}{2}$ tsp cumin seeds
1$\frac{1}{2}$ tsp ground cilantro
2$\frac{1}{2}$ cups stock or water
2 tbsp tomato paste
$\frac{1}{2}$ eggplant, trimmed and cut into $\frac{1}{2}$-in dice
salt
1 x 14-oz can red kidney beans, drained
4 tbsp heavy cream
sprigs of cilantro, to garnish

1 Heat the ghee or oil in a large skillet, add the pork chops and fry until sealed and browned on both sides. Remove from the skillet and reserve.

2 Add the sliced onions, garlic, chilies, ginger and spices and fry gently for 2 minutes. Stir in the stock, tomato paste, eggplant and salt to taste.

3 Bring the mixture to a boil, place the chops on top, then cover and simmer gently over medium heat for 30 minutes, or until the chops are tender and cooked through.

4 Remove the chops for a moment and stir the red kidney beans and cream into the mixture. Return the chops to the skillet, cover and heat through gently for 5 minutes. Taste and adjust the seasoning, if necessary. Serve hot, garnished with cilantro sprigs.

VARIATIONS

Use lamb chops instead of pork chops, if wished. Canned chick-peas and black-eyed peas are also delicious cooked this way in place of the red kidney beans. (Remember to drain them first before adding to the pan.)

STEP 1

STEP 2a

STEP 2b

STEP 3

LAMB & POTATO MASALA

It's so easy to create delicious Indian dishes at home – simply open a can of curry sauce, add a few interesting ingredients and you have a splendid dish that is sure to be popular with family or friends.

SERVES 4

1½ lb lean boneless lamb (from the leg)
4 tbsp ghee or vegetable oil
3 cups potatoes, peeled and cut in large 1 in
    pieces
1 large onion, peeled, quartered and sliced
2 garlic cloves, peeled and crushed
2 ½ cups mushrooms, thickly sliced
1 x 10-oz can Tikka Masala curry sauce, or
    other curry sauce
1¼ cups water
salt
3 tomatoes, halved and cut into thin slices
4 oz spinach, washed and stems trimmed
sprigs of mint, to garnish

1 Cut the lamb into 1 in cubes. Heat the ghee or oil in a large saucepan, add the lamb and fry over moderate heat for 3 minutes or until sealed all over. Remove from the pan.

2 Add the potatoes, onion, garlic and mushrooms and fry for 3-4 minutes, stirring frequently. Stir the curry sauce and water into the pan, add the lamb, mix well and season with salt to taste. Cover and cook very gently for 1 hour or until the lamb is tender and cooked through, stirring occasionally.

3 Add the sliced tomatoes and the spinach to the pan, pushing the leaves well down into the mixture, then cover and cook for a further 10 minutes until the spinach is cooked and tender. Garnish with mint sprigs and serve hot.

SPINACH LEAVES

Spinach leaves wilt quickly during cooking, so if the leaves are young and tender, add them whole to the mixture; larger leaves may be coarsely shredded, if wished, before adding to the pan.

BELL PEPPERS WITH LAMB

This colorful dish can be prepared in advance, ready to cook in the oven when required. Ground beef, pork or chicken can be instead of the lamb, if wished.

STEP 1

STEP 3

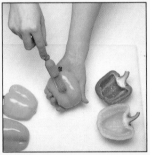

STEP 4a

STEP 4b

SERVES 4-6
OVEN: 375°F

4 tbsp vegetable oil
1 lb lean ground lamb
2 onions, peeled and finely chopped
2 garlic cloves, peeled and crushed
1¹/₂-in piece gingerroot, peeled and finely
    chopped
2 tsp minced chili (from a jar)
1 tsp ground cilantro
1 tsp ground cumin
4 tbsp plain yogurt
2 tbsp tomato paste
2 tbsp chopped fresh mint
¹/₂ cup frozen peas
1 cup canned chopped tomatoes
salt and freshly ground black pepper
3 large red bell peppers
sprigs of mint, to garnish

1 Heat 3 tablespoons of oil in a saucepan, add the lamb and fry until sealed all over. Stir in the onions, garlic, ginger, chili and spices and cook gently for 5 minutes.

2 Stir in the yogurt, tomato paste, mint, peas, tomatoes and seasoning to taste. Cover and cook gently for 15 minutes, stirring frequently. Place in the preheated oven.

3 Meanwhile, cut the bell peppers in half lengthwise, cutting through the stems and leaving them attached. Scoop out the seeds and membranes from each one. Add the bell pepper halves to a saucepan of boiling water and simmer for 5-7 minutes or until only just tender – take care not to overcook them. Drain well, refresh with cold water and drain well again. Pat dry on paper towels.

4 Brush the bell peppers with the remaining oil and arrange in a shallow, greased ovenproof dish. Spoon the lamb mixture into the bell peppers. Cover with greased foil and cook in the oven for 15-20 minutes until piping hot. Serve hot, garnished with mint sprigs.

BELL PEPPERS

A mixture of red, yellow and orange bell peppers really does look most attractive – giving a hot and fiery appearance. If necessaary, to keep the filled bell pepper halves steady in the ovenproof dish during cooking, place them on crumpled aluminium foil.

SPICY BEEF & YOGURT

Deliciously quick and easy – stir-fried steak is served with a tangy eggplant and yogurt dressing. Use mild, medium or hot curry paste according to taste.

STEP 1

SERVES 4

1 lb lean sirloin steak, trimmed
4 tbsp ghee or vegetable oil
2 onions, peeled and sliced
2 garlic cloves, peeled and crushed
2 tbsp mild, medium or hot curry paste
1 tsp minced chili (from a jar)
²/₃ cup beef stock
1cup canned chopped tomatoes

EGGPLANT YOGURT:
¹/₂ medium eggplant
²/₃ cup plain yogurt
1 garlic clove, peeled and crushed
1 tbsp chopped fresh cilantro or parsley
salt and freshly ground black pepper

3 Heat the ghee or oil in a large skillet, add the beef and onions and stir-fry for 5 minutes until the beef is sealed all over.

4 Stir in the garlic, curry paste, chili, stock and tomatoes and bring to a boil. Cover, reduce the heat and simmer gently for 5 minutes, stirring occasionally. Serve hot with the eggplant yogurt.

STEP 2

1 First make the Eggplant Yogurt. Peel the eggplant and cut it into 1-in pieces. Place in the top half of a steamer and steam over boiling water for 10 minutes.

2 Meanwhile, beat the yogurt with the garlic, cilantro and salt and pepper to taste. Allow the cooked eggplant to cool slightly, then mash with a fork. Stir the eggplant into the yogurt.

STEP 3

VARIATIONS

You can use thin strips of pork tenderloin or chicken breast instead of the sirloin steak, if preferred, and serve with Raita rather than Eggplant Yogurt, for a change: see recipe on page 76.

STEP 4

CHAPTER FOUR

Accompaniments

No Indian-style meal is complete without a bowl of fluffy basmati rice, a mixed vegetable side dish (often curried), spicy lentils or at the very least a small bowl of plain yogurt with some diced fruit and vegetables like cucumber, carrot, banana, tomato and onion, often flavored with herbs like mint and cilantro.

Delicately-scented basmati rice, enhanced with the flavor of mild spices, makes the standard accompaniment, but to ring the changes consider coconut rice with its richer and more distinctive coconut flavoring. Mixed vegetable bhajis lend extra variety to a meal as do potatoes cooked with typically Indian spices.

These extras all contribute to give an Indian meal extra flavor and texture. Supplement them with a wide range of ready-made breads like poppadoms, Naan bread (plain or spiced) and stuffed samosas, not forgetting fruity relishes like mango, cooling sauces like Cucumber Raita and pickles with a kick, like lime.

Opposite: Chili peppers drying. Chilies are frequently used in Indian cooking, but be careful to remove the seeds unless you like your food very hot indeed.

STEP 1

STEP 2

STEP 3

STEP 4

AROMATIC PILAU

This rice dish forms the perfect accompaniment to most main courses. It can be prepared ahead of time and reheated in a microwave oven just before serving.

SERVES 4-5

1¼ cups basmati rice
2 tbsp ghee or vegetable oil
1 onion, peeled and chopped
3 cardamom pods, crushed
3 black peppercorns
3 cloves
1 tsp cumin seeds
½ cinnamon stick or piece of cassia bark
½ tsp ground turmeric
2½ cups boiling water or stock
salt and freshly ground black pepper
⅓ cup seedless raisins or golden raisins
½ cup frozen peas
¼ cup toasted, slivered almonds
crisp, fried onion rings, to garnish (optional)

1 Place the rice in a strainer and wash well under cold running water until the water runs clear. Drain well.

2 Heat the oil in a large saucepan, add the onion and spices and fry gently for 1 minute, stirring all the time. Stir in the rice and mix well until coated in the spiced oil, then add the boiling water or stock and season with salt and pepper to taste.

3 Bring to a boil, stir well, then cover, reduce the heat and cook gently for 15 minutes without uncovering. Add the raisins and peas, re-cover and leave to stand for 15 minutes.

4 Uncover, fluff up with a fork and stir the toasted slivered almonds into the mixture. Serve hot, garnished with crisp, fried onion rings, if liked.

SPICES

The whole spices used for flavoring the rice are not meant to be eaten and may be removed from the mixture, if wished, before serving. Simply double up the quantities given for serving 8-10 portions for a party.

STEP 1

STEP 2a

STEP 2b

STEP 3

DAL WITH SPINACH

Lentils are cooked in a delicious blend of spinach, onion, garlic and spices. Okra, also known as bhindi or lady's fingers, are a favorite vegetable in Indian cooking.

SERVES 4

1$^1/_3$ cups lentils
5 cups water
6 tbsp vegetable oil
1 large onion, peeled and chopped
1 leek, trimmed and shredded
6$^1/_2$ cups spinach, stems trimmed and leaves
   coarsely shredded
1 red bell pepper, seeded and chopped
2-3 garlic cloves, peeled and crushed
1-2 tsp minced chili (from a jar)
1$^1/_2$-2 tsp cumin seeds
1$^1/_2$-2 tsp ground cilantro
salt and freshly ground black pepper
mango chutney, to serve

1 Place the lentils in a strainer and rinse well under cold running water. Drain, then place in a saucepan with the water. Cover and cook for 30 minutes until the lentils are tender and the liquid has been absorbed.

2 Meanwhile, heat the oil in a large saucepan and add the chopped onion, leek, shredded spinach and red bell pepper. Fry gently for 8 minutes, stirring and turning frequently until the spinach has wilted. Stir in the garlic, chili and spices and fry gently for a further 2 minutes.

3 When the lentils are cooked, uncover and shake the pot over a moderate heat for a few moments to dry off. Add the lentils to the pot containing the spinach and onion mixture and toss together. Season with salt and pepper to taste and serve hot, with mango chutney.

SPINACH

Fresh spinach is used in this recipe, although frozen leaf spinach (not chopped) may be used instead if more convenient. You require ½ lb frozen spinach, and it should be thawed and squeezed dry before using.

SPICY INDIAN-STYLE POTATOES

Potatoes cooked this way are so delicious, yet quick and simple to prepare. Cut the potatoes into similar-sized pieces to make sure they cook evenly.

STEP 1

SERVES 4

1½ lb potatoes
salt
¼ cup ghee or butter
2 tbsp vegetable oil
1 tsp ground turmeric
1 large onion, peeled, quartered and sliced
2-3 garlic cloves, peeled and crushed
2-in piece gingerroot, peeled and chopped
1½ tsp cumin seeds
¼-½ tsp cayenne pepper
2 tsp lemon juice
1 tbsp shredded mint leaves
sprigs of mint, to garnish

1 Peel the potatoes and cut into ¾-1 in cubes and cook in a saucepan of boiling, salted water for 6-8 minutes or until knife-tip tender (do not overcook). Drain well, return to the pot and shake dry over a medium heat for a few moments.

2 Heat the ghee or butter and oil in a large skillet over medium heat. Stir in the turmeric, then add the sliced onion and the cooked potatoes and fry for 4-5 minutes or until the mixture is beginning to brown, stirring and turning the vegetables frequently.

3 Stir in the garlic, ginger, cumin seeds, cayenne and salt to taste. Fry over gentle heat for 1 minute, stirring all the time.

4 Transfer the potatoes to a warm serving dish. Add the lemon juice to the juices in the pot and spoon the mixture over the potatoes. Sprinkle with the shredded mint leaves, garnish with sprigs of mint and serve hot.

STEP 2a

STEP 2b

POTATOES

This method of cooking potatoes is perfect for using up leftover potatoes – in fact if you've time, parboil the potatoes in advance and leave them to cool before frying for even tastier results.

STEP 4

STEP 2a

STEP 2B

STEP 3

STEP 4

COCONUT RICE

A delicious rice dish flavored with coconut and lemon. For a luxurious touch you can fork through a few shelled, chopped pistachios at the final stage.

SERVES 4-5

1¼ cups basmati rice
3 tbsp ghee or vegetable oil
1 onion, peeled and chopped
2 garlic cloves, peeled and crushed
1-in piece gingerroot, peeled and chopped
½ cinnamon stick or piece of cassia bark
2 carrots, peeled and grated
2½ cups boiling water or stock
salt and freshly ground black pepper
2 tbsp creamed coconut, finely chopped
finely grated rind of ½ lemon or 1 lime
1 tbsp chopped fresh cilantro
1 bunch scallions, trimmed and sliced

1 Place the rice in a strainer and wash well under cold running water until the water runs clear. Drain well.

2 Heat the ghee or oil in a large saucepan, add the onion, garlic, ginger and cinnamon and fry gently for 1 minute. Stir in the rice and grated carrots and mix until well coated with the oil.

3 Stir in the water or stock and season with salt and pepper. Bring to a boil, cover, reduce the heat and simmer gently for 15 minutes without taking off the lid.

4 Add the creamed coconut, lemon rind, chopped cilantro and scallions, fork through and serve immediately.

FOR A SPICIER VERSION

A little garam masala, sprinkled over the rice just before serving adds an interesting "warm" spiciness to this rice dish. If a more fiery flavor is required, fork a little slivered fresh chili (or minced chili from a jar) through the rice in step 4.

MIXED VEGETABLE BHAJI

In this delicious dish, the vegetables are first parboiled and then lightly braised with onions, tomatoes and spices.

STEP 1a

SERVES 4-6

1 small cauliflower
4 oz thin green beans
2 potatoes
4 tbsp ghee or vegetable oil
1 onion, peeled and chopped
2 garlic cloves, peeled and crushed
2-in piece gingerroot, peeled and cut into fine
    slivers
1 tsp cumin seeds
2 tbsp medium curry paste
1 x14-oz can chopped tomatoes
²/₃ cup water
4 tbsp plain yogurt
chopped fresh cilantro, to garnish

STEP 1b

1 Break the cauliflower into neat flowerets. Top, tail and halve the beans. Peel and quarter the potatoes lengthwise, then cut each quarter into 3 pieces. Cook all the prepared vegetables in a saucepan of boiling, salted water for 8 minutes. Drain the vegetables well, return to the pot and shake dry over a low heat for a few moments.

2 Heat the ghee or oil in a large skillet, add the onion, garlic, ginger and cumin seeds and stir-fry gently for 3 minutes. Stir in the curry paste, tomatoes and water and bring to a boil. Reduce the heat and simmer the spicy mixture for 2 minutes.

STEP 2

3 Stir in the parboiled vegetables and mix lightly. Cover and cook gently for 5-8 minutes until just tender and cooked through. Beat the yogurt to soften and drizzle the vegetable mixture with the yogurt. Sprinkle with the chopped cilantro. Serve hot.

POTATO ALTERNATIVES

New potatoes are ideal for this dish because they have a more waxy texture and retain their shape better than main crop potatoes, which, when overcooked, become floury and lose their shape. You could use turnip or pumpkin instead of potatoes, if preferred.

STEP 3

CHAPTER FIVE

Desserts

Indian-style meals are traditionally rounded off with something very sweet or with a large selection of carefully prepared plain fresh fruits like mangoes, guavas, melon and pears. These are best served well chilled, especially in the summer months and can make a welcome change or contrast to a spicy, warm, aromatic main course feast. Dice, slice, or cut the fruit into colorful wedges then arrange them on a huge platter with sprigs of mint for a stunning finale to an Indian meal.

The simplest, and often most appreciated dessert is a cooling Kulfi or ice cream. Many are served plain but others are flavored with mango and coconut and are delicious if sprinkled with chopped shelled pistachios or almonds.

Opposite: A wide selection of delicious fruits are grown in India. Favorite desserts tend to be fresh fruit, fruit salads or ice creams.

INDIAN ICE CREAM (KULFI)

*To make traditional Indian ice cream is quite a time-consuming process,
so why not try this deliciously easy version instead?*

STEP 1

SERVES 6-8

4 cardamom pods, crushed and seeds
   removed
5 tbsp boiling water
1 x 14-oz can sweetened condensed milk
5 tbsp cold water
¼ cup unsalted pistachio nuts
¼ cup blanched almonds
2 drops almond extract (optional)
⅔ cup heavy cream
   lime rind and rose petals, to decorate
   (optional)

1 Pour the boiling water into a
heatproof bowl, stir in the
cardamom seeds and leave for 15
minutes to infuse. Meanwhile, put the
condensed milk into a blender or food
processor together with the cold water,
pistachio nuts, almonds and almond
extract, if using. Process the mixture for
about 30 seconds until very finely mixed.

2 Add the cooled and strained
cardamom water and pour into a
bowl. Whip the cream until softly
peaking and beat into the mixture. Pour
the mixture into a shallow metal or
plastic container and freeze for about 3
hours or until semifrozen around the
edges and mushy in the center.

3 Transfer the mixture to a bowl and
mash well with a fork (to break up
the ice crystals). Divide the mixture
evenly between 6-8 small molds (see
below) and freeze for at least 4 hours or
overnight until firm.

4 To serve, dip the base of each mold
quickly into hot water and run a
knife around the top edge. Turn out onto
serving plates and decorate with lime
rind and rose petals, if using.

STEP 2

STEP 3a

MOLDING THE KULFI

Traditionally this dessert is frozen in
special conical-shaped molds, but you can
use small yogurt pots instead.

STEP 3b

STEP 1

STEP 2

STEP 3a

STEP 3b

MANGO & YOGURT CREAM

*This wonderfully refreshing dessert is designed to help refresh
the palate after a hot and spicy meal.*

SERVES 6

2 large ripe mangoes
2 tbsp lime juice
2 tbsp sugar
²/₃ cup heavy cream
²/₃ cup plain yogurt
4 cardamom pods, crushed, and seeds
   removed and crushed
lime twists or rind, to decorate

1 To prepare each mango, cut along each side of the large central seed, to give 2 halves. Remove the seed, scoop out the flesh and discard the skin.

2 Place the flesh in a blender or food processor with the lime juice and sugar and process until the mixture forms a smooth purée. Turn the mixture into a bowl.

3 Whip the cream in a bowl until stiff, then fold in the yogurt and the crushed cardamom seeds. Reserve 4 tablespoons of the mango purée for decoration, and mix the remaining mango purée into the cream and yogurt mixture.

4 Spoon the mixture into pretty serving glasses. Drizzle a little of the reserved mango sauce over each dessert and serve chilled, decorated with lime twists or rind.

MANGOES

When choosing mangoes, select ones that are shiny with unblemished skins. To test if they are ripe for eating, cup the mango in your hand and squeeze it gently – it should give slightly to the touch if ready for eating.

STEP 1a

STEP 1b

STEP 2a

STEP 2b

AROMATIC FRUIT SALAD

The fruits in this salad are arranged attractively on serving plates with the spicy syrup spooned over.

SERVES 6

3 tbsp granulated sugar
²/₃ cup water
1 cinnamon stick or large piece of cassia bark
4 cardamom pods, crushed
1 clove
juice of 1 orange
juice of 1 lime
¹/₂ honeydew melon
a good-sized wedge of watermelon
2 ripe guavas
3 ripe nectarines
about 18 strawberries
a little toasted, shredded coconut for sprinkling
sprigs of mint or rose petals, to decorate
plain yogurt, for serving

1 First prepare the syrup. Put the sugar, water, cinnamon, cardamom pods and cloves into a saucepan and bring to a boil, stirring to dissolve the sugar. Simmer for 2 minutes, then remove from the heat, add the orange and lime juices and leave to cool and infuse while preparing the fruits.

2 Peel and remove the seeds from the melons and cut the flesh into neat slices. Cut the guavas in half, scoop out the seeds, then peel and slice the flesh neatly. Cut the nectarines into slices and hull and slice the strawberries.

3 Arrange the slices of fruit attractively on 6 serving plates. Strain the prepared cooled syrup and spoon over the sliced fruits. Sprinkle with a little toasted coconut. Decorate each serving with sprigs of mint or rose petals and serve with yogurt, if wished.

VARIATIONS

Use any exotic fruits of your choice, or those that are in season. You can, of course, cut up the fruits and serve them in a bowl, in the usual way, if you prefer.

STEP 2

STEP 3

STEP 4a

STEP 4b

COCONUT ICE CREAM

*This delicious ice cream will make the perfect ending to any Indian
meal. For a smooth-textured dessert, leave out the shredded coconut.*

SERVES 6

¾ cup granulated sugar
1¼ cups water
3½ cups coconut milk
1¼ cups heavy cream
2 tbsp shredded coconut
sprigs of mint or rose petals, to decorate

1 Place the sugar and water in a
saucepan and heat gently, stirring
occasionally until the sugar dissolves.
Boil gently for 10 minutes without
stirring, then remove from the heat and
allow to cool slightly.

2 Mix the cooled syrup with the
coconut milk and pour into a
shallow freezer-proof container. Cover
and freeze for about 3 hours or until
semifrozen around the edges and mushy
in the center.

3 Transfer the mixture to a bowl and
cut up with a knife, then place (half
the quantity at a time) in a food processor
and process until smooth.

4 Turn the mixture into a bowl.
Whip the cream until softly
peaking and fold into the ice cream, then
stir in the shredded coconut. Return the
mixture to the container and freeze again
until solid.

5 Before serving, transfer the
container of ice cream to the
refrigerator and leave in the main
compartment for 30 minutes (or at room
temperature for 15 minutes) to soften.
Scoop or spoon the ice cream into serving
dishes and decorate with sprigs of mint or
rose petals.

SERVING ICE CREAM

For easy serving, scoop the ice cream into
portions the night before required and
place on a chilled baking sheet, then
freeze until ready to serve.

BANANAS WITH SPICED YOGURT

Golden saffron and delicate cardamom add an exotic flavour to this quick and easy dessert that is a good end to almost any meal.

STEP 1

SERVES 4-6

3 good pinches saffron strands
2 tbsp whole milk
6 cardamom pods, crushed and seeds
    removed and crushed
3 tbsp butter
3 tbsp soft brown sugar
1/2 tsp ground cinnamon
2 bananas
2 cups plain yogurt
2-3 tbsp honey, to taste
1/4 cup toasted, slivered almonds

mixture on top of the bananas and liberally sprinkle the surface of each serving with toasted, slivered almonds. Chill before serving, if preferred.

STEP 1a

1 Place the saffron strands on a small piece of foil and toast very lightly under a hot broiler. Crush the saffron strands finely and place in a small bowl. Add the milk and crushed cardamom seeds, stir well and leave to cool.

2 Meanwhile, melt the butter in a skillet, add the brown sugar and cinnamon and stir well. Peel and slice the bananas and fry gently for about 1 minute, turning halfway through cooking. Remove from the skillet and place the fried banana slices in decorative serving glasses.

STEP 2a

ALTERNATIVE

The flavor of saffron strands is improved by lightly toasting before use, but do take care not to overcook them or the flavor becomes bitter. This delicious dessert may also be made using half cream and half yogurt, and the tops can be sprinkled with unsalted, chopped pistachios instead of almonds, if wished.

3 Mix the yogurt with the cold spiced milk and the honey. Spoon the

STEP 2b

INDIAN COOKING

TASTY ACCOMPANIMENTS

Below is a selection of deliciously easy accompaniments to serve with your Indian dishes.

Apple and onion relish Peel, core and coarsely grate 1 large cooking apple into a bowl. Add ½ bunch chopped scallions, 2 tsp vinegar or lemon juice, 1-2 tsp sugar, to taste, and ½ tsp roasted cumin seeds. Mix well and chill before serving, sprinkled with chopped fresh cilantro.

Radish and cucumber yogurt put 2½ cups plain yogurt into a bowl and season with salt and freshly ground black pepper. Stir in ½ bunch trimmed and coarsely chopped radishes, ¼ unpeeled, diced cucumber, 1 small chopped onion and 1-2 tbsp chopped fresh mint. Serve chilled.

Cucumber raita Mix 2½ cups plain yogurt with ⅓ peeled and grated cucumber. Season with salt, freshly ground black pepper and a pinch or two of cayenne pepper. Just before serving, dry-roast 1 tsp cumin seeds, then crush coarsely and sprinkle over the yogurt mixture. Add a little finely chopped fresh mint to the mixture, if wished.

continued opposite

It's never been easier to create quick and authentic tasting Indian dishes thanks to the marvelous range of exciting spices, tempting ingredients and ready-prepared products available in supermarkets and specialty grocery stores. All the ingredients used in the recipes in this book are easy to find from the larger supermarkets.

SPICES

Spices play an essential part in Indian cooking, but don't be put off by the vast array of jars and packages on the supermarket shelves. Remember that you only need a few to give characteristic flavor to your Indian cooking.

It is best to buy whole spices (they keep their flavor and aroma much longer than the ready ground spice) and to grind them as you need them. A small coffee grinder or a mortar and pestle does the job easily. If you cook a lot of Indian dishes, it may well be worth grinding the various spices in small quantities at a time: store them in small, airtight containers and use up quickly.

When time is short, however, do make the most of the ranges of commercially prepared products in supermarkets. Spice mixtures such as curry powders, garam masala and tandoori spices and the jars of ready-made curry pastes and so on are extremely convenient and make light work of adding flavor and authenticity to Indian-style dishes. Useful too, are the jars of minced chilies and chopped fresh

gingerroot – and the varied selection of canned curry sauces (ranging from mild to medium and hot) ensure there is something to please most palates.

Here is a suggestion of just a handful of spices well worth buying to give your Indian meals that special flavor and aroma:

Cardamom These small pods contain numerous tiny black seeds which have a warm, highly aromatic flavor – green cardamoms are considered the best. Cardamom pods (used in savory and sweet dishes) are often lightly crushed prior to adding to dishes to allow the full flavor of the seeds to be appreciated.

When the whole or crushed pods are used they are not meant to be eaten and should either be removed before serving or simply left on the side of the plate by the diner.

When the seeds only are required, the pods should be lightly crushed to break them open and the seeds removed for using whole or crushed, according to the recipe. Use a mortar and pestle or the end of a rolling pin for crushing either pods or seeds.

Cinnamon Available in stick and ground form. Shavings of bark from the cinnamon tree are processed and curled to form cinnamon sticks, and these will keep almost indefinitely in an airtight container. This fragrant spice is used to flavor savory and sweet dishes and drinks. The sticks are not edible and should be removed before serving, or may be used as a garnish or decoration.

Cassia Cassia comes from the bark of the cassia tree. It is not as uniform in shape as cinnamon sticks, but has a similar, although less delicate flavor.

Cilantro An essential spice in Indian cooking, cilantro has a mild and spicy flavor with a slight hint of orange rind. It is available as seeds or ground.

Cloves These dried unopened flower buds are used to give flavor and aroma to foods, but should be used with care as the flavor can become overpowering. When whole cloves are used they are not meant to be eaten and may be removed before serving, if wished.

Cumin These caraway-like seeds are used extensively in Indian dishes, either in their whole or ground form. Cumin has a warm, pungent and aromatic flavor.

Garam masala This is a ground aromatic spice mix that generally includes cardamom, cinnamon, cumin, cloves, peppercorns and nutmeg. It may be used during and toward the end of cooking, or sprinkled over dishes as an aromatic garnish just before serving. You can buy this spice ready-mixed or prepare your own quite simply: finely grind together 1 tsp each black peppercorns and cumin seeds with 1 tbsp cardamom seeds, 8 whole cloves, a 2 in piece of cinnamon stick or cassia bark and about ¼ teaspoon freshly grated nutmeg. Store the mixture in an airtight container and use within 3

weeks. This quantity makes about 3 tablespoonfuls.

Ginger Fresh gingerroot is now widely available from supermarkets and gourmet stores. It looks like a knobbly brown stem and should be peeled and chopped, sliced or grated before use. It is also available minced in jars.

Paprika This ground, bright red pepper, although similar in color to fiery cayenne pepper, has a mild flavor and is used for coloring as well as flavoring dishes.

Saffron This spice (the most expensive of all) has a distinctive flavor and gives a rich yellow coloring to dishes. It is available in small packages and jars, either powdered or in strands – the strands have by far the better flavor.

Turmeric Is an aromatic root which is dried and ground to produce a bright, orange-yellow powder. It has a warm, distinctive smell and a delicate, aromatic flavor. It is frequently used to give dishes an attractive yellow colouring.

CHILIES

Fresh chilies, used extensively in Indian dishes to give them their hot and fiery flavor, vary considerably in size, shape and hotness – it really depends on the variety. It's worth remembering that all chilies are hot, so use caution when adding them to a dish. It is wise to start with small amounts – you can always add more to taste at a later stage according to personal preference. Take

Tasty Accompaniments continued.

Carrot, raisin and onion salad
Coarsely grate 1½ cups carrots into a bowl. Peel and quarter 1 onion, cut into paper-thin slices and add to the carrots. Stir in 3 tbsp seedless raisins and 1 tbsp lemon juice. Season with ¼ tsp paprika, ½ tsp grated fresh gingerroot, salt and freshly ground black pepper. If wished, add slivers of fresh chili (or a little minced chili, from a jar) for a more fiery flavor. Mix all the ingredients well together and leave to stand for 30 minutes before serving, to allow time for the flavors to develop.

DRINKS

When serving spicy dishes be sure to have a supply of refreshing drinks to hand – chilled mineral water, iced water or fruit juice are excellent choices. For special occasions and for a deliciously refreshing drink to sip during a hot, spicy meal, serve iced water flavored with spices, such as cardamom, cumin, cassia or cinnamon. Wine is not good served with Indian foods, because the taste is overpowered by the strong flavors of the food, so opt instead for chilled beers. You could also provide a pitcher of Lassi – the delicious Indian drink of lightly spiced yogurt which is designed to cool the palate.

To MAKE LASSI: Put 2½ cups plain yogurt in a blender or food processor with 6¼ cups cold water, 1-2 tsp lemon juice, 1 tbsp chopped fresh mint, ½ tsp each salt and dry-roasted cumin and freshly ground black pepper to taste. Blend for about 1 minute, then serve in a pitcher or tall glasses filled with crushed ice.

To MAKE SWEET LASSI: Omit the lemon juice, mint, salt, cumin and pepper and instead flavor the yogurt and water with sugar, ground cardamom and a little rosewater, to taste. Blend well and serve over crushed ice.

care too, when preparing chilies. The cream-colored seeds inside are the hottest part and may be removed before using, if wished; generally, the seeds are only left in if you like your spicy dishes very hot! Chilies contain a pungent oil which can cause an unpleasant burning sensation to eyes and skin, so it is advisable to wear thin rubber gloves when handling them, and to be sure not to touch your face or eyes during preparation.

To prepare a chili: cut the chili in half lengthwise, cut off the stem end, then scrape out the seeds with a pointed knife and discard. Rinse the chili under cold running water and pat dry before chopping or slicing as required. Once you have finished, thoroughly wash your hands, utensils and surfaces with soapy water.

Dried red chilies are sold whole or ground and are used to make cayenne pepper and chili and curry powders. Again, remove the seeds from dried chilies. Chili powders come in varying degrees of strength, so check the label before you buy, as many are a blend of chili and other spices, such as "chili seasoning" – a popular blend that is quite mild.

You can also buy minced red chili in a jar from many supermarkets – this is an excellent and most convenient way of adding a fiery touch to Indian dishes without any hassle.

Green chilies, too, are available in brine or pickled in sweetened vinegar – these should be drained and dried on paper towels before using.

FRESH CILANTRO (DHANIA)

This pretty green herb has leaves rather similar in appearance to flat-leaf parsley. It is frequently used in Indian dishes both as a garnish and for its delicate flavor.

COCONUT

Many Indian dishes are flavored with coconut. The ready prepared shredded type is convenient and easy to use, however, you really do get the very best flavor from fresh grated coconut. It freezes well, too, so is well worth preparing to freeze in handy quantities to use when required.

To prepare for freezing: choose a fresh coconut that is heavy with liquid (best way to check is to give it a good shake before buying). Break it in half, drain off the liquid and prise the coconut from its shell. Using a potato peeler, peel off the brown skin and break the flesh into small pieces. Place in a food processor and process until finely grated, or, if preferred grate larger pieces on a cheese grater. Freeze in small, usable quantities for up to 3 months. It thaws quickly and can be used as required.

Creamed coconut is sold in bars at Asian grocery stores. It is broken into pieces and reconstituted with boiling water.

Coconut milk, made from water and coconut meat too, is a popular ingredient in Indian cooking. It's available in cans, or as a powder in sachets, to make up into a liquid following the package instructions.

You can also make your own delicious version very easily: chop creamed coconut (see above) and place in a heatproof measuring jug. Pour in enough boiling water to come to the 2½ cup mark and stir until dissolved. Cool and use as required. This will keep in the refrigerator for up to 1 week.

GHEE

Indian recipes often call for ghee (or clarified butter) for cooking. It can be cooked at high temperatures without burning and gives a delicious rich, nutty flavor to all manner of dishes and a glossy sheen to sauces. You can buy ghee in cans from Indian food stores– and a vegetarian ghee is also available. Vegetable oil may be used instead of ghee, as preferred.

RICE

The two types of rice most frequently used in Indian cooking are ordinary long-grain rice and basmati rice, which, although rather more expensive, is prized for its slender grains and fine aromatic flavor. This is the one to use whenever possible, but if you can't afford this variety every time, save it for special occasions.

It is essential to rinse rice, particularly basmati, in a strainer under cold running water, before cooking to get rid of the starchy residue left from the milling process. Easy-cook rice always gives good results. It is also now possible to buy brown basmati rice, which will take a little longer to cook.

YOGURT

Homemade yogurt (dahi) is used extensively in Indian cooking for marinading meats and poultry to tenderize and flavor them, and also as an ingredient in various dishes and sauces. It is also widely used as a cooling accompaniment to spicy dishes, such as Raita, see recipe on page 76. A brief stir before using will thin the consistency, if necessary. Any plain yogurt of your choice may be used, if preferred.

SUPERMARKET ADDITIONS TO A HOMEMADE INDIAN MEAL

There's a wonderful selection of ready-prepared products available from some supermarkets and Asian grocery stores that you could include with your homemade dishes. A basket of poppadums, for example, is always favorite as an appetizer. Other traditional and popular accompaniments could include parathas, chapatis or naan, plus a bowl of yogurt or Raita (see page 76) and a selection of pickles or chutneys, such as lime or mango.

DRINKS TO SERVE
You will need a supply of cooling and refreshing drinks to accompany an Indian meal – the best ones are ice-cold water, chilled beers and fruit juices. Fine wine is wasted because the taste is overpowered by the strong flavors of the food.

DAL

Dal are actually split peas, lentils and beans. There are several different kinds available, which can all be used to make the dal that you will find on the menu in Indian restaurants.

$1/3$ cup chana dal or yellow split peas, soaked
5 cups water
$1/2$ tsp turmeric
1 onion, chopped
1 tsp ground cumin
2 tbsp vegetable oil
$1/2$ tsp mustard seeds
2 garlic cloves, crushed
2 dried chilies, seeded and chopped
1 cup canned chopped tomatoes
salt and pepper

1. Drain and rinse the lentils, then place in a saucepan with the water and turmeric. Bring to a boil then cover and simmer for 30 minutes.

2. Add the onion and cumin, stir, cover and cook for another 15 minutes.

3. Meanwhile, heat the oil in a small skillet and add the mustard seeds. When the seeds pop add the chilies and tomatoes. Cook for 2-3 minutes, then add the contents of the skillet to the lentils. Stir well, add salt and pepper to taste and serve.

INDEX